boyzone

a different story

Copyright © 1997 UFO MUSIC LTD

UFO Music Ltd
18 Hanway Street London W1P 9DD England
Telephone 0171 636 1281
Fax 0171 636 0738

First published in Great Britain 1997
UFO Music Ltd
18 Hanway Street London W1P 9DD

The author and publishers have made every
effort to contact all copyright holders. Any who
for any reason have not been contacted are
invited to write to the publishers so that a full
acknowledgment may be made in subsequent
editions of this work.

ISBN 1-873884-89-3

Designed by UFO Music Ltd

boyzone

a different story

Melissa Field

Ronan

Steve

Mike

Keith

Shane

introduction

Ronan Keating. Stephen Gately. Mikey Graham. Shane Lynch. Keith Duffy. If those five ordinary names mean more than *anything* to you, chances are you call yourself a Boyzone fan. You're not alone. The Irish fivesome are without doubt the most successful pop band in the world today. But why do we love them so much? Yeah, it's got a lot to do with their great music, their fit bodies and gorgeous smiles and the fantastic excitement and exhilaration we feel when we see them on TV or in concert. But Boyzone have got something more. Something that makes them that extra bit special. They truly love their fans. They're all genuinely nice guys. The sort of guys you'd love to hang out with, go out with, whatever. They're five ordinary guys made good. This is their story....

chapterone
THE STORY SO FAR...

When five ordinary Irish lads calling themselves Boyzone arrived on the British pop scene less than three years ago many people had their doubts. Some said they were merely another talentless manufactured boyband. Others argued that many bands before had tried to take on the mighty British fab fivesome Take That and failed miserably. Why should Boyzone be any different? Even the lads themselves knew that their dream, to achieve international pop success and respect, wouldn't come easily.

But Ronan, Stephen, Mikey, Shane and Keith had qualities that the doubters and critics hadn't counted on. Determination, Guts, Ambition, and Talent - by the bucket load. They were certain that - with just a tiny bit of luck - they would make it. No matter what *anyone* said.

So began the wonderful journey. Like any journey to success, the beginnings were humble. The first step was to make it at home. That meant travelling the backroads of Ireland in a beaten up transit van. Three gigs a day - every day. A school at lunchtime. A village hall in the early evening. A nightclub at midnight. Then back on the road. Day after day after day. This band would be no overnight one hit wonder. A year on the road finally saw the boys rewarded with their first hit single. Their version of The Detroit Spinners classic *Working My Way Back To You* charted at Number 3 in Ireland. That success was quickly followed up by the lads' first Number 1, a soulful cover of The Osmonds *Love Me For A Reason*. At last they had proved their critics, mainly moaning old rock bods, wrong. Ireland *would* accept a hunky pop fivesome. Now it was time to take on the world.

The lads arrived in Britain in November 1994. It was like starting all over again. Back home in Ireland, they were national heroes. They were mobbed if they so much as nipped out for a newspaper and fans camped on their doorsteps night after night. Many would have been content with that level of success in their home country. Not Boyzone. They were out to conquer the world. Time for phase two. A month was set aside solely for the notoriously sceptical British press. The lads spent day after day doing phone interviews, photo shoots, radio shows and P.A's (personal appearances). The schedule was exhausting but after the experience they had gained in Ireland they knew that this was the only way to get to the top.

They needn't have worried. Anyone whoever met the boys (this writer included) was impressed by their charm, honesty and friendliness. Not to mention their downright sexy good looks! In short, Boyzone were like a breath of fresh air and their time had come. Magazine after magazine ran stories and cover features on the new Irish phenomenon and within days readers began demanding to know when and where they could buy a Boyzone single or see them perform. When the first British single *Love Me For A Reason* was released it debuted at Number 10, climbing to Number 2. This was an incredible achievement. Not only were Boyzone the first Irish band to chart in Britain with their first ever single release, they'd managed to do it during the highly competitive Christmas period. Only East 17's magnificent *Stay Another Day* kept Boyzone off the prestigious Christmas Number 1 spot. Not that it mattered. So far Boyzone's success had gone way, way beyond even their wildest dreams.

With the release of *Key To My Life* early in 1995, Boyzone at last proved that they were more than a bunch of all-singing and all-dancing pretty faces. The song was written by Mikey, Ronan and Steve and showed that Boyzone contained songwriters of real talent and maturity. It charted at Number 3. *Back For Good*, (widely considered Take That's masterpiece) was Number 1. That was followed up by another smoochy, dreamy ballad *When All Is Said and Done* and an upbeat funky little number *So Good*. Both charted highly. Finally Boyzone released their debut album *Said and Done* which, not surprisingly topped the album charts. Success in Europe, the Far East and Australia was also beckoning. If 1994 had been a good year for Boyzone, it looked like 1995 would be a corker! Obviously a number 1 single in the UK

boyzone

would be the icing on the cake. The boys decided that the best weapon in their arsenal was *Father and Son*, a cover of the Cat Steven's classic. Again the lads took a risk and aimed for the Christmas Number 1. They so very nearly got there too. Not that they considered a long spell at Number 2 by any means a failure - after all - King Michael Jackson kept them off the top spot, and The Beatles were *below* them at Number 3.

Despite the incredible achievements of the past two years, the Boyzone boys each had little voices deep down inside telling them that 1996 would be their year. Sure, 1995 had seen them grab great chart positions, magazine covers, nationwide tours and the hearts of more and more female fans, but 1996 would be THE YEAR of Boyzone. And

they weren't wrong. The release of the corking spring single *Coming Home Now* coincided with the break up of Take That. The Kings of Pop crown was Boyzone's for the taking. It was well and truly theirs when they finally got the one thing that had eluded them - a number 1 single with *Words*. Meanwhile, Mikey and Keith had extra reason to celebrate in '96 when they both became dads. Some people thought that having two dads in Britain's premier pop group might turn the fans off but Mikey and Keith weren't

going to hide the fact that they were now proud daddies. They needn't have worried. The fans were nearly as excited with the guy's new roles as Mikey and Keith themselves and showered them both with a deluge of toys and letters when Jordan (Keith's little boy) and Hannah (Mikey's daughter) were born.

Boyzone grew up in 1996. They commenced their first ever British stadium tour and had another number 1 single *A Different Beat.* and their second album (also called *A Different Beat*) hit the top spot.

Over the past three years, you've probably sung Boyzone's songs with your mates, while thinking about loved ones or even while doing mundane chores, like homework or tidying your bedroom. You've probably fallen in love with one or all of the boys (I know I have!) Already they've become a part of your histories. Boyzone are going to be with us for a long, long time yet. They haven't worked this hard to throw it all away by falling out or splitting up.

And while their incredible journey has brought them this far, there's still a lot of road left to travel yet. But one thing's for sure - the loyal fans (just like you....) that they've gathered all across the world will be travelling it with them. For always....

chaptertwo
ALL ABOUT Steve

Little Stephen Gately is Boyzone's premier boybabe. He's gorgeous and loveable in a sexily sweet kind of way. But what turns him on? What turns him off? What makes our favourite pop babe tick? To find out everything you ever wanted to know about sweet Stephen, read on...

NAME	*Stephen Patrick David Gately.*
BORN	*March 17 1976 (St Patrick's Day!)*
STARSIGN	*Pisces.*
AGE	*Twenty one.*
HEIGHT	*5 foot 7 inches.*
LIVES	*North Strand, Dublin, Ireland.*
ANY MORE AT HOME?	*Stephen has three brothers, Mark, Tony and Alan and a sister Michelle.*
GIRLFRIEND	*Nope, Steve is single.*
PETS	*Did have a pet dog called Sting but sadly he died last year.*
WHO DOES HE FANCY?	*Supermodel Cindy Crawford.*
STEPHEN DESCRIBES HIMSELF AS	*'Caring, loving, mysterious, quiet and unpredictable.'*

When Stephen was a little boy, he had a dream. He wanted to be a star. It wasn't the usual sort of dream for a boy growing up in inner-city Dublin but Steve was determined. One day, he would be famous and nothing, but nothing was going to stop him.

"Since I was about nine I was determined to be famous, no matter what." he explains. *"I just felt that I had to do that because there's no one famous in my family and I said to myself 'I'm going to be the first famous Gately in the world!'"*

So instead of playing football in Seville Place, the street where he grew up or hanging out with his mates, Steve took himself off to dance classes.

It soon became clear that little Stephen Gately was a talented lad. He took as many classes as he could and was soon encouraged to add voice training and acting classes to his busy schedule. He was on the way to

STEPHEN GATELY

13

achieving his dream.

His first break came when he landed a blink-and-you'll-miss-it cameo role in hit Irish flick *The Commitments*. It didn't matter. It was a start and Stephen was ecstatic. His appearance in the hit movie lead to a stream of modelling offers. Six years of long hard slog was paying off. Stephen was as ready as he'd ever be for stardom. All he needed now was the Big One. His chance to prove he could be a star.

That chance arrived when the Irish newspaper *The Star* ran a small ad looking for five talented lads to form a band. The only problem was Stephen didn't see the ad. He very nearly missed the opportunity that was to change his life forever!

Luckily for Steve a mate had spotted the ad and mentioned it to him a couple of days later. Most people would have let it slide. Accepted that they were probably too late to be in with a chance. Not our Stephen. Somewhere, deep down inside, he knew that this was the moment he'd been waiting for so he rang the newspaper and begged to know more. Who could he contact? Where were the auditions? Had the band been formed? A sympathetic journalist dug out the information and passed the details on to a grateful Stephen.

The good news was that Stephen was just in time. Auditions would be taking place at trendy Dublin nightclub The POD later that week. The bad news was that 300 other hopefuls showed up, all as desperate as Steve for a crack at stardom. Despite his fear and nerves, Steve didn't let the other hopefuls put him off. He told himself over and over that this was his chance, he'd worked for it and he deserved it. As he stepped up to the mike for his audition, he took a deep breath, crossed his fingers and began. His first choice was an old favourite, *Hello* by Lionel Richie. Steve's rendition of the smoochy ballad impressed John Reynolds and Louis Walsh, the men who would soon be managing Boyzone. His second number was *Right Here Waiting* by Richard Marx. By the time Stephen started to dance, there was no doubt. He was in.

The Boyzone whirlwind took off straight away and while Stephen was loving every minute of it (after all, it's what he had wanted all his life) he did have to grow up pretty quickly. The hardest thing for Stephen to cope with was the travel. Steve was a homeboy at heart and Boyzone's constant tours and promo appearances - so vital if the band were to succeed - took their toll. He missed his mam. He ran up huge mobile phone bills by phoning home every day and earnt himself the nickname Homeboy.

"I ring my mum everyday and when I go home my family are like, *'Make us a cup of tea Stephen'*, or *'Go down the shops for us'*. Things like that keep your feet on the ground."

Thankfully, Steve has overcome his homesickness now, although he still rushes home to Dublin whenever he can. He's enjoying his celeb status, particularly as he's the fans favourite. Not that his incredible popularity has gone to his modest head of course. *"I'm not so sure I get more fan mail than the rest of the lads."* he says softly. *"I just know that I get a lot!"*

Stephen is a genuinely nice guy. He takes time to personally write back to fans who've written him poems and letters or sent gifts and will stop and chat to anyone. And one thing's for sure, despite craving fame for so long, now that he's achieved it he hasn't let his stardom go to his pretty head. *"I keep down to earth by chatting to people. I love a good natter. I ring my mum everyday and when I go home my family are like, 'Make us a cup of tea Stephen', or 'Go down the shops for us'. Things like that keep your feet on the ground."*

But what about love? Stephen is undeniably gorgeous but his busy timetable allows little time for L.O.V.E. *"I'd love to have someone to snuggle up with,"* he explains. *"But it's very very hard to keep a relationship going when you're travelling as much as we are. I'm going to wait until the band is over before I get involved with someone seriously. I'm not in any rush."* When that time comes, Steve will be looking for a girl next door type. *"I like natural looking girls, curly brown hair and I love big brown eyes. The most important thing though is that she's outgoing, cheerful and happy."*

Just like Stephen himself.

chapterthree
ALL ABOUT Mikey

Mikey is Boyzone's broodingly handsome father figure. Whenever the other lads have got a problem they know exactly who they can turn to. Mikey is serious, thoughtful and wise with an abundance of talent. This is his story.

NAME	*Michael Christopher Charles Graham.*
BORN	*August 15 1972.*
STARSIGN	*Leo.*
AGE	*Twenty Four.*
HEIGHT	*5 foot 11 inches.*
LIVES	*Coolock, Dublin.*
ANYMORE AT HOME?	*Five sisters, Yvonne, Avril, Kathy, Claire and Debbie and one brother, Niall.*
GIRLFRIEND	*Yep. Mikey's got a girlfriend called Sharon and an eight month old baby daughter Hannah.*
PETS	*Family pet sheep dog called Peppy.*
FANCIES	*Kylie Minogue.*
MIKEY DESCRIBES HIMSELF AS	*'Strong and silent but fun!'*

Mikey Graham is a complex character. As the oldest boy in the 'Zone (he's an ancient 24!) he's seen by the fans as the quiet sensible one. The one who keeps an eye out for the rest of the lads. The one the older fans and mums fancy! But don't be mistaken into thinking that he's Boyzone's spare part. Without Mikey, there wouldn't *be* a Boyzone.

That's because Mikey is Boyzone's chief songwriter and of all the lads, his background is the most firmly rooted in music. His large boisterous family were all music mad so Mikey needed no encouragement to pursue his interest in all things musical. At the age of five he joined Billy Barry's School in Dublin to study dance and drama. At eight, he picked up his first guitar and started writing little songs and tunes. By the time he was 15 Mikey had left Billy Barry's School and was fronting his own band Ivory. Music had become Mikey's life.

"I got the inspiration to play guitar and write songs from listening to people like Eric Clapton and Sting." he explains. *"Soul based music. In fact,*

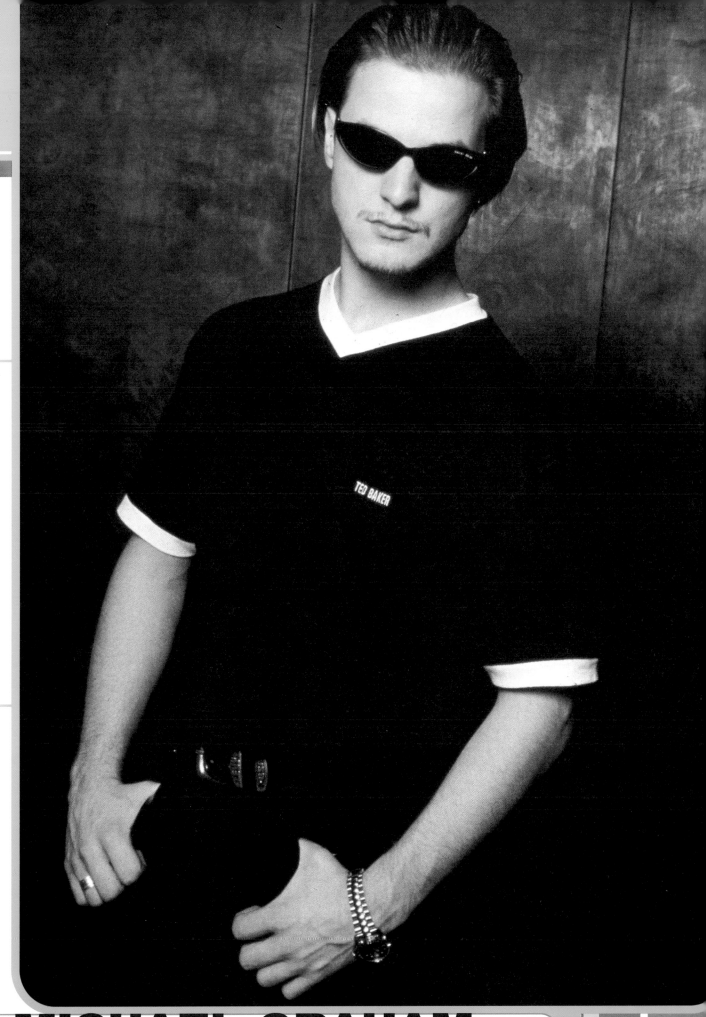

MICHAEL GRAHAM

I wrote a lot of songs before the band came together and now I try and write songs that will suit the band."

When Mikey wasn't singing, writing songs or playing with his band he was training to be a mechanic. But he had no desire to spend the rest of his life underneath other people's flash cars. Like the rest of the lads, he had a feeling deep down that one day he would be famous in some way. It wasn't that he craved a glamourous popstar life - apart from maybe a flash car or two! - but he knew that he wanted more and that nothing anyone said or did was going to stop him. *"Lets face it,"* he says, *"There are a lot of bums out there who don't want to better themselves. I do and so I'm not going to let their criticism get to me."*

The Boyzone audition was Mikey's chance to go for gold. He made the fab five - but only just. *"I was the last one knocked out of the audition. I was disappointed when I didn't get into the band but I had a feeling that it didn't matter."* He was right. After original members Richie Rock was sacked and Mark Walton left, managers John and Louis Walsh remembered Mikey's talent and invited him to join, just weeks after he'd received his rejection letter. He was in.

Mikey's determined and fiercely ambitious. He also admits that he's got a terrible temper which he tries to keep in check. He revealed these qualities in Boyzone's early days when he said, *"The lads and me are out to win. We're not out to be a one hit wonder. What's the point when we have the capability of being so much more?"* How right he was.

Nowadays, Mikey has an extra reason to ensure that Boyzone remain at the top. His daughter Hannah. He admits that when long-term

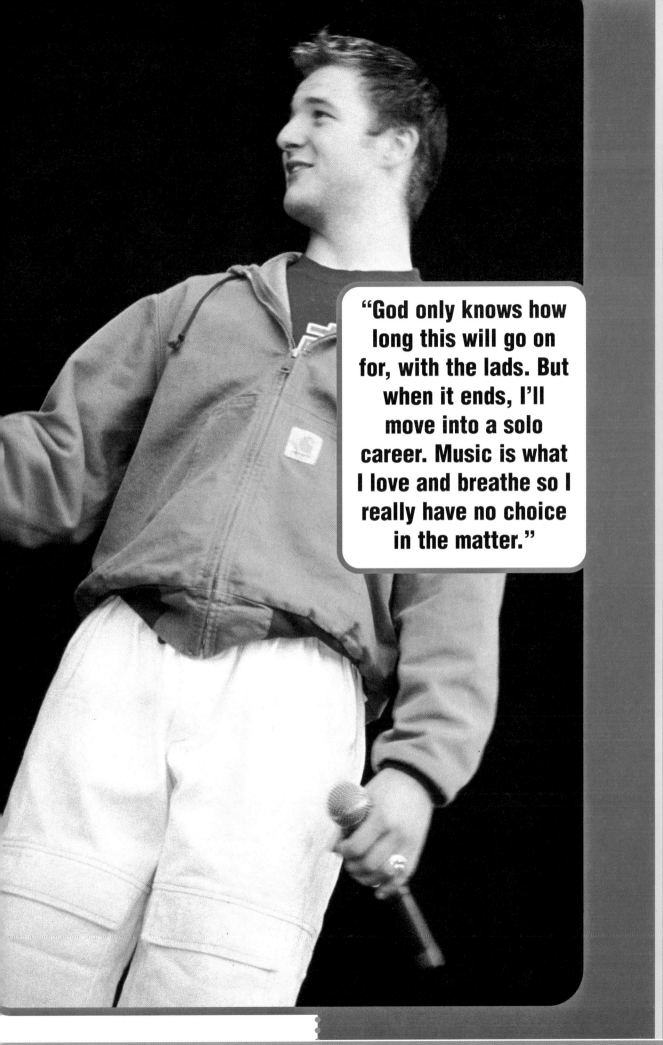

"God only knows how long this will go on for, with the lads. But when it ends, I'll move into a solo career. Music is what I love and breathe so I really have no choice in the matter."

on-off girlfriend Sharon announced she was pregnant, he went into a complete state of shock. His emotions were all over the place and because the pregnancy was unexpected, he wasn't even sure he was ready to become a dad. As he got used to the idea, his feelings changed. Now he says, *"Becoming a dad isn't something I can describe in words. In all the madness surrounding Boyzone my daughter is the only sane thing I have and I'm madly in love with her."* In fact, like any new daddy, Mikey's gone quite goo goo over his little girl. *"She's my precious little angel and I speak to her on the phone everyday - even though she can't talk yet!"*

Mikey's managing to combine pop stardom with fatherhood. When he's not racing home to Dublin to spend time with his girlfriend and daughter he says he loves nothing more than giving his all on stage. *"I love performing. I wait all day for those 90 minutes on stage. That's why we're here, it's why we do what we do."*

So what of the future? Mikey hopes Boyzone will be around for a good five years or so yet. *"God only knows how long this will go on for, with the lads. But when it ends, I'll move into a solo career. Music is what I love and breathe so I really have no choice in the matter."*

chapterfour
ALL ABOUT Shane

Seriously sexy Shane is an easygoing lad who likes a laugh. But is that all there is to this Boyzone babe? No way, Shane is a self confessed shy guy who takes his time getting close to someone. Here's where we get close to Shane.

NAME	Shane Eamonn Mark Stephen Lynch.
BORN	3rd July 1976.
STARSIGN	Cancer.
AGE	Twenty.
HEIGHT	6 foot 1 inch.
LIVES	London, England and Grange, Dublin.
ANYMORE AT HOME?	Shane shares his London flat with Ronan. Back in Ireland, he's got six sisters, Tara, Keavy, Catherine, Naomi, Adele and Allison.
GIRLFRIEND	Officially no, but was strongly rumoured to be dating Easther from Eternal.
PETS	Not at the mo. Used to own a garter snake called Caesar until his mum made him get rid of it.
FANCIES	Melanie Griffifths.
SHANE DESCRIBES HIMSELF AS	'Shy, sensitive, controlled, fearless and easy going.'

Once upon a time there was a rowdy lad who loved nothing better than tinkering with cars and motorbikes. He'd spend hours in his dad's garage, getting greasy, underneath the bonnets of different cars, learning how they ran and how to mend them when they didn't. His name? Shane Lynch.

Shane's dream was to be a motor mechanic. He didn't have much time for school. In fact he spent more time bunking off than in class and eventually his school headmaster thought it best if he were to leave. According to him, Shane was nothing but a time wasting poser! Shane couldn't have been happier. At last he could spend all his time with his beloved cars and bikes. He even told his parents that rather than being

SHANE LYNCH

"I don't consider myself a babe magnet at all. I've always had this fear of being rejected if I really liked somebody. I've never had the confidence to approach a girl."

expelled from school (i.e.: the truth) he'd decided to leave himself so he could take up his mechanics apprenticeship. They were happy. They knew that their son Shane was a stubborn yet determined lad and that he was better off pursuing his dream.

But Shane had another dream. As he worked on his cars and bikes in his dad's cramped garage, he'd listen to music. He'd sing to himself and occasionally dance. New Kids On The Block were massive at the time and Shane began to think to himself 'I could do that...' Shane's dad would encourage him. As his son sang over his work in the garage he would say to Shane *"Go for it son, you should get into that, get it together"*

But Shane wasn't one for joining dance classes or drama schools. When he wasn't messing about with cars he liked to hang out with his mates. Not surprisingly, sexy Shane was a popular lad and spent his spare time hanging out in pubs and clubs. More often than not, his mate Keith Duffy (sound familiar?) was by his side. Keith lived round the corner from Shane and the pair met when Keith briefly dated one of Shane's sisters. Both their lives were to change on one ordinary night.

Shane was dancing in a club, just having a laugh with his mates when he spotted Louis Walsh, the man who would become Boyzone's manager. Shane had vaguely thought about phoning him up and suggesting that they form an Irish Take That. Somehow he'd never got around to it. But now his chance was here. Despite his self assurance, cockiness even, Shane is a shy lad deep down so it took him some courage to approach Louis. But he did it. The pair had a brief chat and Shane thought no more of it. Until a week later when he saw the ad that Louis placed in The Star.

Boyzone was Shane's idea but he still had to audition alongside the other 300 lads. He admits he panicked. *"I was totally taken aback by the experience of those guys. Some of them had sung in bands. I didn't know if I had the right to be in that room."*

For Shane, the audition process went right down to the wire. He made it to the last ten. But there was no need to worry. Despite the fact that the only real singing he'd done was a brief stint in the school choir and round his dad's garage, it soon became clear that Shane had a great voice and he was a demon dancer. That combined with his drop dead good looks ensured that his spot in the line up was guaranteed. Shane was in.

To Boyzone fans, Shane is the outrageous, sexy one. The sort of fella mum's and dads are wary of. A bit of a bad boy. However, appearances can be deceptive. Despite his fitter than fit bod, jet black hair and piercing blue eyes, Shane is not the ladykiller he appears to be. In fact he insists that really, he's a shy boy and a one woman man to boot! *"I don't consider myself a babe magnet at all. I've always had this fear of being rejected if I really liked somebody. I've never had the confidence to approach a girl."*

If that's the case, it's a good job that Shane is now an internationally famous popstar. Why? Because that means he gets to mix with

boyzone

27

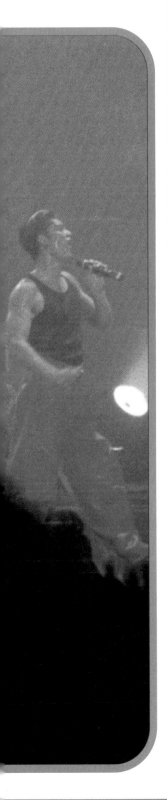

other, internationally famous *female* popstars. In particular a certain Easther Bennett of Eternal fame. For the last year, it has been strongly rumoured that the pair a have been a hot item. So is it true? Shane smiles. *"I'm not denying the fact that I go out with Easther....but I go out with Louise too, we're all good friends and I have a lot of female friends."* He's not giving anything away. As for Louise, the pair are definitely great mates. They'd have to be. They share a flat in London's Chelsea along with Ronan Keating.

Not that they get to spend many cosy nights in together watching EastEnders. Their busy schedules ensure that it's rare they're all in for the night together. So what does Shane like to get up to on a rare night off then? *"When I'm home in Dublin I don't go out much. All I do is go and race cars. Just around the back streets. I do it at night so we don't hit pedestrians or kids. There's about five of us who do it and we burn each other off at the lights. It's me hobby. "* (Not one we recommend *you* try at home though!)

Shane's not much of a party animal these days either. On the lads recent arena tour, Shane admits he was tucked up in bed early every night. Well, nearly every night. *"I can't handle drinking anymore. I was alright at the start of the tour but by the middle I needed me sleep cos we work so hard."*

Another thing Shane can't handle is the falseness rife in showbiz. In fact he's even had a tattoo done to remind him. *"There's a lot of back biting in this business."* he explains, looking thoughtful. *"When people in this biz first meet someone, immediately they have something to say about them and to me that's just not right. My tattoo translates as 'Do Not Judge Or You To Will Be Judged.' It means a lot to me. People judge other people far too easily."*

It seems Shane's learnt a lot over the past four years with Boyzone. When it's all over, he knows exactly what he wants to do. *"When this ends, I'll get married, settle down in Ireland. I'll invest in property, tinker with me cars and live happily ever after."*

boyzone

chapterfive
ALL ABOUT Keith

Anyone's who's ever been lucky enough to be in the same room as hunky Keith will already know everything there is to know about this Boyzone boy. How so? Cos he would have told you. Keith loves a chat and will talk to anyone about anything. Here's the low down on a certain Keith Duffy...

NAME	*Keith Peter Thomas John Duffy.*
BORN	*October 1 1974.*
STARSIGN	*Libra.*
AGE	*Twenty Two.*
HEIGHT	*6 foot.*
LIVES	*Dublin.*
ANYMORE AT HOME?	*Yep. Two brothers Derek and John.*
GIRLFRIEND	*Keith lives with his girlfriend Lisa and their baby son Jordan.*
PETS	*Family pet dog called Socks and a rabbit called Shoes.*
FANCIES	*Michelle Gayle.*
KEITH DESCRIBES HIMSELF AS	*'A hard man who's full of life with a heart of gold.'*

Keith Duffy is Boyzone's chief party animal. In fact, on the lads recent UK tour, Keith managed to rack up a £6,000 bar bill. But don't worry, Keith's not turned to drink to help him cope with Boyzone's incredible fame. Being the generous, sociable fella he is, he just couldn't resist partying every night with mates like Sean Maguire and Ant and Dec. That's Keith all over, a great laugh to be with and generous with it.

Keith's always been the sort of guy everyone wants to hang out with. After all, he's good looking, great fun to be with, and he could talk the leg off a chair. If there's one thing in the world Keith likes to do it's have a good old natter.

But was Keith always like this? It seems so. As a schoolboy growing up in Donaghmede, Dublin, he loved to play in the streets with his large group of mates. He loved Gaelic football and when he was really little, he

KEITH DUFFY

loved to play Cowboys and Indians in his back garden. One of his earliest childhood memories is getting a wigwam (a sort of Indian tent) and Indian costume for Christmas when he was about four. *"It was never off me back!"* he says with a laugh.

At school Keith or *'Duffster'* as he was known by his mates, was immensely popular. But he didn't have too much time for schoolwork. He admits that the last time he opened a book was when he had to read The Hobbit for school when he was 15. Even so, Keith did well and went on to college to study architecture. There was just one small problem. Like the rest of the Boyzone lads, Keith had a feeling, deep down inside that an ordinary life wasn't for him. He wanted something different and exciting for himself, he just didn't know what it was. With that instinct nagging his mind, Keith chucked in his architecture course two weeks into his second year - even though he came top of the class after the first year.

He got a job as a waiter and spent long afternoons working on his already spectacular body in the gym. At night, he would go clubbing with his large gang of mates (including Shane Lynch). Keith was well known around Dublin clubs because he was a brilliant dancer. Keith loved clubbing and dancing so much he needed another job to fund his social life. On the quiet, he got a job as a strip-o-gram. He never told his mum where his extra dosh was coming from and she never found out until Keith found fame with Boyzone. She only discovered the truth when a national newspaper phoned her up for an

interview and asked her what she thought of her son, the popstar who used to strip for a living! *"It was hilarious!"* says cheeky Keith, *"Me mam started bawling and me dad laughed his head off. I promised I'd never do it again."*

Lucky for Keith, no harm was done. In fact, it could be said that Keith's experiences as a male stripper helped him nab a place in the fab five.

Keith was dancing in a club when Louis Walsh spotted him. He invited Keith to join him in the VIP lounge for a drink and asked him to audition for the boyband he was putting together. Keith went along to the final audition and sang *Piano Man* by Billy Joel. It was the only song he knew all the words to because his dad used to sing it around the house. Then he was asked to dance to *I'm Too Sexy* by Right Said Fred. He couldn't believe his good luck. He'd made up a routine to that very song just weeks before because he'd had to do a strip-o-gram to that same tune. *"I think that's what got me the gig."* he says with a laugh.

Keith admits he's not the band's strongest singer but says *"I can hold a note and I know I'm not ugly so in many ways that's enough to be at least one of the members of a band like Boyzone."* Most importantly, Keith discovered, first with his stripping and then on stage with Boyzone that he loved to entertain. He'd finally found that *'something'* he'd been looking for when he gave up college.

Like bandmate Mikey, Keith's got an extra reason to ensure Boyzone remain at the top. His girlfriend Lisa gave birth to a son Jordan a year ago and Keith knows that continuing mega-

"I can hold a note and I know I'm not ugly so in many ways that's enough to be at least one of the members of a band like Boyzone."

success with Boyzone is the best way he can provide a safe future for his son. Even if that means sacrificing time with little Jordan. *"The band is my priority in life, everything else is number two."* he says with a glint of steely determination in his eye. *"My career has to be more important cos I have to secure a future for my child. I go home as often as I can and I miss him like mad when I'm away."*

Keith admits that his job is hard on his girlfriend Lisa. *"She's knows what I'm like, up partying every night while she's up with the baby."* Still Keith got to do his fare share of nappy changing when Lisa and Jordan joined the last Boyzone tour for four days. So was his son a fan of his daddy's band? *"We let him watch the show though he had earplugs in. It was so sweet because we made him up his own laminate with his picture on and he smiled all the way through the show."*

With fans that young, it looks like Keith will be in a job for a good while yet!

chaptersix ALL ABOUT Ronan

Boyzone's baby is adored by fans young and old. It's no surprise. He's a lovely guy who'd most likely make the world's perfect boyfriend. Find out everything you ever wanted to know about the 'Zone's most luscious lad here!

NAME	*Ronan Patrick John Keating.*
BORN	*3rd March 1977.*
STARSIGN	*Pisces.*
AGE	*Twenty.*
HEIGHT	*5 foot 10 inches.*
LIVES	*Chelsea, London and Swords, Dublin.*
ANYMORE AT HOME?	*Three brothers, Gary, Gerard and Kieran and a sister, Linda. Ronan's the baby.*
GIRLFRIEND	*He says no but v. strongly rumoured to be dating Vernie Bennett from Eternal.*
PETS	*None.*
FANCIES	*Vernie from Eternal!!*
RONAN DESCRIBES HIMSELF AS	*'Sensitive, paranoid, honest, happy and quiet.'*

When a young lad is kicked out of his junior school choir because it's thought he can't sing, not many people would expect that same lad to grow up to became one of the world's hottest popstars. But that's exactly what happened to Ronan Keating, Boyzone's youngest member. ***"I wasn't actually kicked out,"*** he admits, laughing. ***"But the choir teacher just never invited me back so I got the hint. I should go back and see her now shouldn't I?"***

Absolutely. Ronan's had incredible success with Boyzone. Along with Stephen he's probably the 'Zone's most lusted-after boy. He writes songs with Mikey and Stephen and he sings lead vocals on most Boyzone tracks. He's certainly gone a long way to proving his old choir teacher wrong eh?

Not that he ever let others doubts put him off. Ronan had always acted and sang in local and school productions. And if you think he only penned his first song since joining Boyzone you'd be wrong. Ronan wrote his first song during his first year at secondary school and went on to form a

RONAN KEATING

"I will never leave
this band. I don't know
what I'd do without the
other lads, I love it so
much. Boyzone is my
life and I'm incredibly
lucky."

band called Nameste with some mates in his year. They played in the school gym at lunchtimes and by all accounts were rated highly, particularly their angelic lead singer Ronan!

While Ronan enjoyed school for the time he got to spend with his mates and working with the band he had little time for actual study or work. *"I hated school,"* he says with a shudder. *"I just never paid attention. I also got into one or two fights."* Despite his babyfaced good looks it seems Ronan was not quite the angel he appears. In fact, his school days came to a bit of a sorry end. Ronan explains. *"I got caught cheating on an exam which was pretty nasty. It was an end of year exam and I had the book open on my lap. When I got caught, I just knew I couldn't go back."*

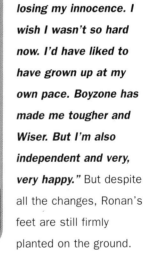

Ronan must have a guardian angel watching over him because after the exam fiasco and before he was due back at school he auditioned for Boyzone. He impressed Louis Walsh with his rendition of the Cat Steven's classic *Father and Son* . So much so that *Father and Son* was the B-Side to the lads first Irish single *Working My Way Back To You* and later released as a single on its own. (It charted at Number 2.) Ronan got the gig and - provided his parents agreed- he'd never have to go back to school again. There was just

one small problem. Ronan's mum was dead against the idea. *"She was afraid I'd get into drugs and play at night in all kinds of shady clubs,"* he admits. But Ronan had a talent that couldn't be denied. Finally she agreed and Ronan was on his way.

Life has changed a lot for Ronan over the past four years. As Boyzone's baby, at times it has been difficult for him to cope. *"In some ways, I've changed a lot since I've been in the band,"* he says thoughtfully. *"I regret losing my innocence. I wish I wasn't so hard now. I'd have liked to have grown up at my own pace. Boyzone has made me tougher and Wiser. But I'm also independent and very, very happy."* But despite all the changes, Ronan's feet are still firmly planted on the ground. *"I want to be normal. On tour, I carry my own bags. At home I sweep the floor and still go down the shops for me mam. The only difference between me and another bloke my age is the job I do. I have a great job!"*

And he also gets to mix with *great* female stars. Not that Ronan's dishing any dirt. He firmly denies that he's dating Eternal's Vernie. *"We're just good friends,"* he insists. *"We've gone to some shows together and we have gone out to dinner. We just hang out together. We're mates*

with all the Eternal girls but there's no relationships there." He also shares a London pad with bandmate Shane and the lovely Louise. And while he admits that "Louise is a lovely girl and she'd make a lovely girlfriend," he also insists that it's not often they all stay in for a cosy night together. "We don't see much of each other actually. We only share for convenience. Ant and Dec live in the same block and we don't see them either."

Ronan's come a long way with Boyzone but he knows there's still a long way to go. In the beginning, all the boys dreamt of doing an arena tour and having a number one single. Now that they've achieved both those aims, Ronan's after his next goal. Respect. "I'm really looking forward to being respected some day. Take That did it, they had respect from the industry. I suppose it may take awhile for Boyzone but I feel like we're making steps in the right direction." One things for sure, Ronan's in for the long haul. "I will never leave this band. I don't know what I'd do without the other lads, I love it so much. Boyzone is my life and I'm incredibly lucky."

chapterseven
IN THE STARS

A man's starsign and birthdate can tell us a lot about his character, his life and loves and his future. Boyzone are no exception. By taking a look at the lads' birthdate and starsign we can unlock Boyzone's personality secrets and discover what the future holds for our favourite five.

Steven

BIRTHDATE	March 17 1976.
STARSIGN	Pisces.

CHARACTER

As a Piscean, our Steve is a dreamy and creative kind of guy. An ordinary existence working nine to five would be very bad for his health. There's nothing that he loves more than time on his own, thinking things over and dreaming about the future. He's the sort of guy that sees the beauty in all things around him, even if it's just a little flower or the smell of freshly baked bread. As a Piscean, Stephen is at his happiest when he's composing music or writing songs.

LOVELIFE

Stephen may be single right now but being the gentle, honest and caring guy he is, he's got a lot of love inside to give. Whoever eventually receives that love will be a very lucky lady indeed. Stephen wouldn't dream of being unfaithful and will make a very romantic partner. He's a one woman man and when he commits to someone, he commits for life. Stephen takes love so seriously he probably won't settle down for a few years yet. He'll wait until he's absolutely positive he's met The One.

LOVEMATCHES

Aquarian, Gemini, Sagitarian or Pisceans.

THE FUTURE

Stephen has achieved incredible success at such a young age. While he loves it now, in a few years time, he may want a change of pace. He'll want to settle down in one place and make a home for himself. That said, it's unlikely he'll disappear from view altogether. An acting career looks likely. A very successful one too.

mikey

BIRTHDATE	15th August 1972.
STARSIGN	Leo.

CHARACTER

Mikey's birthdate and starsign indicate that he's the sort of guy who's main ambition in life is to be happy. He wants a happy family life, well balanced relationships with family, friends and partners and a job that he enjoys. The thought of being bored frightens him so he's very ambitious to succeed in his career. He can be quiet and thoughtful at times and if something upsets him he can get depressed quite easily. With those that he trusts, he can be the life and soul of the party. A man with many sides. Mikey is an interesting kind of guy who'll only reveal his true self when he's known you for a good long while. He's also unfailingly honest.

LOVELIFE

If he's in the mood, he can be the world's biggest flirt. He'll chat and pay compliments, focusing his attention completely on the object of his desires. If he's not in the mood however, you won't even know he's in the room, he'll keep to himself or stick with his mates. In love, he's a faithful and romantic sort. Expect flowers and chocolates - and not just on Valentine's day either. They say still waters run deep and Mikey's no exception. He's extremely passionate.

LOVEMATCHES

Taureans, Virgoans, Leos and Gemini's.

THE FUTURE

Talented and ambitious, Mikey will continue successfully in the music biz once Boyzone are finito. He'll probably take a more behind-the-scenes role, in production or songwriting which will suit him just fine.

shane

| BIRTHDATE | 3rd July 1976. |
| STARSIGN | Cancer. |

CHARACTER

Outwardly boisterous and rowdy this is merely a disguise for a sensitive soul. Shane is the sort of guy that gains a lot of confidence by having a large circle of friends around him at all times but he feels most comfortable amongst close pals. He's always taking in those around him and always gives people a chance to prove themselves. He doesn't quickly form an opinion about those around him but as an excellent judge of character , he's nearly always right when he finally does. Shane makes a great mate and friendship is very important to him.

LOVELIFE

When he's young, he takes advantage of being young free and single. Not in a nasty way, it's just that he doesn't believe there's any point in settling down too early. He believes it's best to go out with lots of different girls, that way, he'll know when he's met Miss Right. He's very open minded. She may be the girl next door, a girl who lives abroad or even a fan. Whoever she is, she'll have to be strong and independent. Shane can't bear clingy companions.

LOVEMATCHES

Scorpios, Leos, Aquarians and Taureans.

THE FUTURE

Once Boyzone is over, Shane will make the most of the financial success he's achieved with the group. He'll live like a king, following his dreams. Race rally cars, travel the world, build his dream home (In Dublin of course) and settle down with his dream girl. It would be no surprise to find that after all his searching, she's someone he's known for years and years. Whatever he does, he'll do it with a great big smile on his gorgeous face, that's for sure.

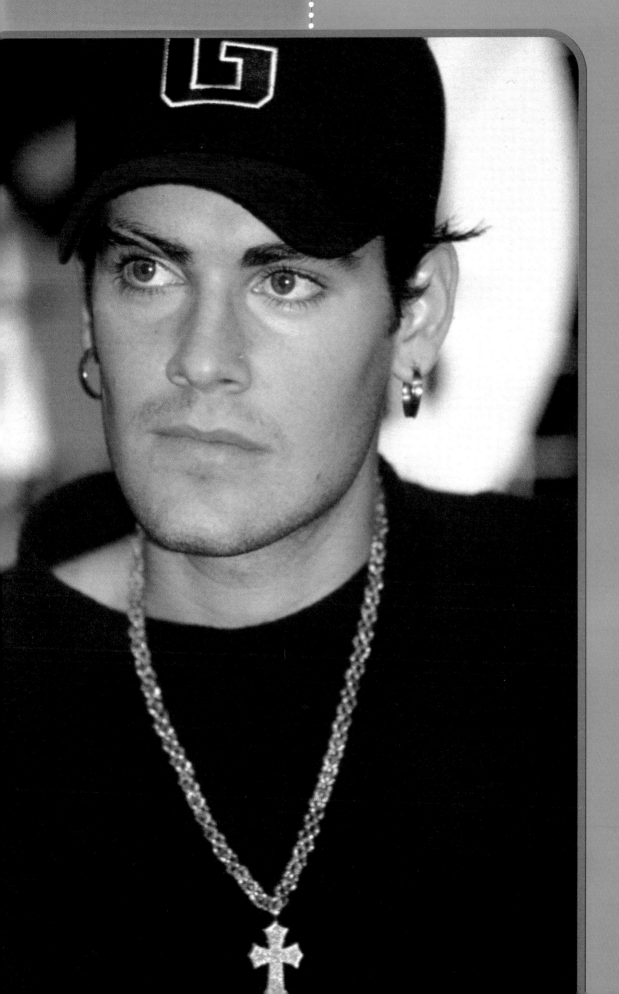

Keith

BIRTHDATE	1st October 1974.
STARSIGN	Libra.

CHARACTER

Keith is every inch the Libran. Strong, boisterous, sensual and ambitious, he's destined to do well in life. Keith's birthdate indicates a man who loves success, has masses of drive and will go all out to achieve what he wants in life. He can go a bit over the top at times. A popular character, he loves nothing more than socialising, talking and entertaining. Despite that, he's desperate for stability at home and his home is his refuge. Only very very close friends get an invite into his personal space.

LOVELIFE

Keith is a very sexy, very sensual type of guy. He's extremely tactile and passionate and isn't shy about showing love and affection. His idea of heaven is a long slow massage and long slow kisses. Saying that, he's also extremely possessive. Any partner who makes the mistake of betraying Keith by being unfaithful would be cut out of his life without a second thought. Keith's got quite an old fashioned view of love. He likes to take care of his partner. He sees himself as the strong manly one, it's his job to care for his lover. He'll give his all for the one he loves, and he expects the same in return.

LOVEMATCHES

Librans, Ariens, Cancerians and Scorpio's.

THE FUTURE

Very very bright. Keith will work his little cotton socks off to keep Boyzone at the top. He'd never dream of quitting the band. When it does all come to an end, he'll probably take a year or two off, travel the world with his partner and his kids and then finally settle down.

ronan

BIRTHDATE	3rd March 1977.
STARSIGN	Pisces.

CHARACTER

On the surface, Ronan seems shy sweet and quiet. But deep down he's got a fierce determination and a bit of a tough streak. He won't let anyone tell him what to do or walk all over him. He's very protective of those he loves and a very trustworthy friend. If you went to Ronan with a problem, he'd give the matter his serious consideration and then come up with a brilliant way to deal with the dilemma. He knows what he wants out of life and nothing will stop him going for it. He's got a great love of the good things in life, be they food, drink, music or clothes. He's also extremely generous with his cash.

LOVELIFE

Ronan would make an absolutely ideal boyfriend. He's got very high moral standards and firmly believes in the idea of love. In that case, he doesn't give his heart to love easily, he's got to be sure that he's really in love before he'll commit to anyone. Once he has, he makes a thoughtful, considerate and caring partner, willing to put his all into the relationship.

LOVEMATCHES

Cancerians, Taureans, Sagitarians and Virgoans.

THE FUTURE

Ronan has a long future ahead of him, almost certainly in the music business. He'll definitely go solo when the band ends and achieve a high level of success on his own. Boyzone is his life at the moment so it's highly unlikely he'd ever leave the band. He won't settle down with a partner for a good few years yet because when he does, he'll be committing for life.

chaptereight
50 BOYZONE SECRETS

Over the past three years, we've come to know and love the fab five. But everyone's got their secrets. Even the Boyzone lads. We uncover 50 of the best!

1. Ronan believes that if anyone was going to leave Boyzone it would be Mikey. Not that he's going anywhere it's just that Mikey has admitted in interviews that Boyzone is a stepping stone to a solo career.

2. Mikey's dream is to be a mechanic who plays in a rock band and lives in New York - after Boyzone of course!

3. Shane could speaks fluent Portuguese - his family used to holiday there every year so that's how Shane picked up the lingo.

4. After his experiences as a strip-o-gram Keith says he'd pose nude but this time he'd have to be paid at least £50,000!

5. On tour, the lads insist that their dressing room snacks include a bowl of raspberries, a basket of crisps and mini chocolate bars, lots of banana's, lots of water and some honey and lemons.

6. Ronan had his first kiss at the age of 13. He says it frightened the life out of him because he didn't know what was going on.

7.   If there's one question Ronan hates being asked it's *'How did Boyzone get together?'*. So if you bump into him down the shops one day, DON'T ask him that!

8.   Keith's favourite on tour nosh is boiled gammon while Mikey enjoys tucking into a plateful of mashed potatoes.

9.   Ronan and Shane always share hotel rooms on tour.

10. Steve's favourite tourbus video's include *The Lion King*, *The Shawshank Redemption* and *Die Hard With A Vengeance.*

11. Shane's taken up a new hobby - skateboarding.

12. All the lads love boiled cabbage. Urgh!

13. Ronan always brushes his teeth with a white toothbrush.

14. Shane first began plucking his eyebrow when he was 17. He says it doesn't hurt anymore.

15. If Ronan wasn't called Ronan, he'd like to have been named Levi, Summer or Brandon.

16. Shane does 100 sit ups every night - even if he's been in the bar with the lads!

17. Nowadays Ronan drives a swank popstar BMW, but his first car was a slightly less glam Opal Astra.

18. Stephen says the popstar he would most like to snog is Janet Jackson. Why? *'Because she just looks really really soft!'*

19. Keith would want Brad Pitt to play him in a film about his life.

20. Before Mikey settled down with girlfriend Sharon, his favourite chat up line to use was *'You are beautiful.'* Very direct!

21. Last year Shane bought his dream car - a Porsche.

22. Keith also owns a Porsche but drives around Dublin in a painter and decorators van so he doesn't get recognised.

23. Mikey admits that occasionally he has a problem with smelly feet. But he says that *'at least I don't do bottom burps all the time like the rest of the lads.'*

24. Stephen once had a crush on 24 girls - all at the same time! He had to change schools as a youngster and was put in a class that contained only one other boy plus 24 girls. *'I was in love with every one of em', it was wonderful,'* he says with a smile!

25. Stephen's favourite present from a girlfriend was a *'beautiful John Rocha (swank Irish designer) sweater. I still wear it all the time.'*

26. Ronan refuses to go onstage unless he's got his lucky mascot on him. What is it? A plaster on his right index finger.

27. Shane once had a crush on his history teacher. He says she was about 74!

28. Keith is short sighted but he won't get his eyes checked in case he's forced to wear glasses.

29. When Boyzone is over, Shane fancies having a go at professional rally car driving.

30. Mikey checks into hotels under a false name. The last one was Mike Drake after Dracula. Spooky.

31. Shane wears boxer shorts in bed and sleeps with one leg outside the covers. He admits he talks in his sleep but Mikey reckons he snores.

32. Keith once bunked off school for a week - to sunbathe. He got caught out when his mum wanted to know how he got such a good suntan!

33. Before he settled down with his girlfriend, Mikey admits he was a bit of a ladies man. He once snogged eight girls in one night!

34. Stephen goes to sleep with the telly on.

35. One of Ronan's favourite places in the world is St Patrick's Cathedral on Fifth Avenue in New York. He likes to sit there and think.

36. The lads favourite concert venue is The Point in their hometown, Dublin.

37. Everyone knows that Ronan could have been a champion runner. He won the Under 13 All Ireland championships. But did you know his favourite race was the 400m and that he was offered an athletics scholarship in New York?

38. Shane's natural haircolour is a mousy brown. He's dyed it black since he was 15.

39. When the lads were playing at The Point in Dublin last year Steve's trousers split. Embarrassingly, his trews were black and his undies were white so the split could be spied from the back row!

40. Stephen's really got into going to the theatre. Last year alone he saw *Phantom of The Opera*, *Sunset Boulevard*, *Martin Guerre*, and *Les Miserables*.

41. Mikey's pet hate is the powerful camera flashes on photo shoots. *'They wreck me eyes, and wreck me head. But they're an occupational hazard.'*

42. Steve's favourite game when he was little was *Operation*. *'It's the boardgame where you have to use tweezers to pick out the different body parts. I was really good at it!'*

43. Shane's got a bit of a thing about older women. As well as lusting after Melanie Griffifths, he really fancies Madonna too.

44. Ronan doesn't like fans camping outside his house or hotel room - but only cos he worries about them. *'Sometimes I'm cold in my room, I really worry for them when their outside and it's freezing. I also worry that their not safe either.'*

45. A few years ago, Robbie Williams said some rather nasty things about Boyzone lads, including telling a gathering of the world's press that *'Boyzone weren't very good at all really'*. It's a good job Keith's a forgiving kind of guy. The pair are now the best of mates!

46. Having two trained motor mechanics in the band has come in handy on a couple of occasions for Boyzone. Both Shane and Mikey made repairs to the lads transit van when it broke down as they travelled around Ireland in the early days. Well done lads.

47. As a child, Mikey had angelic white blonde hair. Aww.

48. Boyzone are an accident prone bunch of lads. Ronan gashed his head just hours before he was due to appear on Irish television in Boyzones first ever television appearance. Shane broke his ankle jumping over a low wall and Mikey severely injured his neck when he fell off a horse whilst filming a documentary with the lads.

49. We all know Keith's a cheeky lad but did you know that his girlfriend Lisa was actually going out with his best mate before Keith started dating her.

50. Shane's a bit of a wheeler dealer. He once spotted a set of old tyres in a deserted garden. They'd been there so long, weeds were growing through the tyres. That didn't stop Shane taking them home, cleaning them up and then selling them on to a mate for £100!

chapternine
QUIZZONE

If you're truly Boyzone bonkers this tantalisingly teasing quiz should prove no problem.

1. Shane once had a pet snake. What was it called?
   a) *Julius*
   b) *Marcus*
   c) *Caesar*

2. Which Boyzone babe once earnt himself the nickname Homeboy cos his missed his mammy so much on tour?
   a) *Steve.*
   b) *Keith.*
   c) *Ronan.*

3. When Boyzone's managers were advertising for lads to form the band that became Boyzone, which Irish newspaper did the ad appear in?
   a) *The Sun.*
   b) *The Telegraph.*
   c) *The Star.*

4. Which film did Steve have a blink-and-you'll-miss-'im role?
   a) *Mission Impossible.*
   b) *The Commitments.*
   c) *The Lion King.*

5. On their last tour, what name did Mikey check into hotels under?
   a) *Mike Drake.*
   b) *Mike Snake.*
   c) *Mike Rake.*

6. Which two lads always share a room when they're on tour?

a) *Mikey and Steve.*

b) *Shane and Steve.*

c) *Ronan and Shane.*

7. Ronan was rumoured to be dating which gorgeous pop babe?

a) *Vernie Bennett from Eternal.*

b) *Louise.*

c) *Gabrielle.*

8. Keith became a daddy this year. What's his girlfriend's name and what's his little boy called?

a) *His girlfriend is called Lisa and his son is called Jordan.*

b) *His girlfriend is called Louise and his son is called Johnny.*

c) *His girlfriend is called Lily and his son is called Jake.*

9. When Keith's little boy had been born, what magazine did he, his girlfriend and his son appear in?

a) *OK*

b) *Alright!*

c) *Hello!*

10. What does Shane always take on tour with him?

a) *A picture of his family.*

b) *A picture of his car.*

c) *A picture of his house.*

11. When Mikey was at school, he fronted his own band. What were they called?

a) *Ebony.*

b) *Amber.*

c) *Ivory.*

12. Which boy would love to have a hot snog up with Janet Jackson?

a) *Stephen.*

b) *Ronan.*

c) *Mikey.*

13. Keith, Ronan and Steve wear Calvins, Mikey wears Armani - what underwear does Shane wear?

a) *A G-string.*

b) *Designer Y- Fronts.*

c) *He doesn't wear any!*

14. Shane and Ronan share a swanky popstar pad. Where is it and who do they share it with?

a) *It's in Dublin and they share with Robbie Williams.*

b) *It's in London's Chelsea and they share with Louise.*

c) *It's in London's Chelsea and they share with Robbie Williams.*

15. What does Keith drive around Dublin to avoid recognition?

a) *A Milkfloat.*

b) *A Robin Reliant.*

c) *A painters and decorators transit van.*

boyzone

61

16. Whose favourite fruit is bananas?

   a) *Mikey's.*

   b) *Shane's.*

   c) *Stephen's.*

17. Last year, Boyzone advertised a breakfast cereal. Which one was it?

   a) *Sugar Puffs.*

   b) *Rice Krispies.*

   c) *Special K.*

18. Mikey's girlfriend gave birth to a daughter last year. What's her name?

   a) *Harriet.*

   b) *Hannah.*

   c) *Helga.*

19. Who says his sexiest feature is his lovely long curly eyelashes?

   a) *Stephen.*

   b) *Shane.*

   c) *Ronan.*

20. Ronan drives a rather swanky popstar car. What is it?

   a) *Mercedes.*

   b) *Ferrari.*

   c) *BMW.*

21. If Ronan found Aladdin's lamp, what would he wish for?

   a) *Perfect teeth!*

   b) *To be taller.*

   c) *To be able to speak French.*

22. Boyzone got to number 1 last year with their single *Words*. Who originally recorded that song?

   a) *Abba.*

   b) *The Bee Gees*

   c) *The Beatles.*

23. The lads first hit single in Ireland was:

   a) *Working My Way Back To You.*

   b) *Love Me For A Reason.*

   c) *Key To My Life.*

24. What was Keith studying at college before he left?

   a) *Medicine.*

   b) *Graphic Design.*

   c) *Architecture.*

25. When Stephen goes to bed at night, he snuggles up in:

   a) *Nowt - he likes to snooze in the nude!*

   b) *His boxer shorts - he doesn't like to get too hot in bed.*

   c) *His fluffy jim jams.*

boyzone

ANSWERS.

1 - c   2 - a   3 - c   4 - b   5 - a

6 - c   7 - a   8 - a   9 - c   10 - b

11 - c   12 - a   13 - a   14 - b   15 - c

16 - c   17 - a   18 - b   19 - b   20 - c

21 - a   22 - b   23 - a   24 - c   25 - b

How to Score
It's so simple! Just give yourself a point for each correct answer.

0 - 11
While there's no doubt whatsoever that you are well and truly Boyzone bonkers, it looks like you spend more time drooling over gorgeous pictures of the lads than reading up on them. But hey, who can blame you. You're the sort of fan so struck by the lads sheer gorgeousness you haven't got *time* to read all about 'em. This book should help you gen. up on the fit fella facts!

12 - 20
Very good. You've certainly done your homework on the lads but could improve your knowledge of their intimate info by reading this book one more time. That way you'll pick up all those key facts you missed. Just try not to spend to long gazing at the luscious pictures, if possible!

21 - 25.
What can we say, you seem to know more about Boyzone than the boys themselves. Nothing can phase you - you know everything there is to know about the lads and can only be called a Superfan of the highest degree. Well done!